Leadership

The Best Ways To Inspire Our Team Members And Help
Them Grow Professionally Via Dialogue, Instruction, And
Evaluation

*(Gain Financial Freedom Through The Use Of
Mathematical Intelligence)*

MuhamedReisner

TABLE OF CONTENT

Introduction

Although not everyone has the innate ability to lead, everyone can do so with effort and willpower. You may become an effective leader if you have the proper guidance.

This book offers tried-and-true methods for becoming a successful leader, including how to interact with your team and inspire and motivate them, among other things.

You may become a successful leader and pave the way for success in your business and other endeavors by reading this book!

Be the best leader you can be by reading this book right now.

I appreciate you downloading this book once more, and I hope you enjoy it!

The purpose of this document is to give accurate and trustworthy information on the subject and problem discussed. The publication is marketed under the false impression that the publisher is exempt from providing officially authorized, qualified, or accounting services. A qualified practitioner should be consulted if legal or professional counsel is required.

- From a Declaration of Principles that both a Committee of Publishers and Associations and an American Bar Association Committee recognized and approved in equal measure.

3

Reacting to Other People

The ability to respond to others appropriately is a crucial social skill. In order for there to be effective communication, a leader must both talk and permit others to speak. He responds appropriately when others say. Thus, a leadership trait is reacting to people in a discourse. A leader's reactions are typically characterized by decency, civility, politeness, and dignity. An abusive leader is going to be around for a short time.

Kinds of answers.

Using questions, remarks, and exclamations are all forms of responding as a communication tool. Asking a speaker a question demonstrates your interest in the topic and want to learn more. Comments show your awareness of the issue, your degree of expertise about it, and your desire to add something to the discussion. Your contributions enhance the debate about whether they are directly relevant to the topic at hand or have a more tangential connection. Exclamations convey astonishment, dismay, or agreement with what has been said while demonstrating that you have been paying close attention to what the others are saying.

Opposition.

Reacting in a social communication style involves disagreeing with the ideas and viewpoints that other people have stated. A leader needs to be able to clearly articulate his perspective and separate the wheat from the chaff. Therefore, feel free to disagree as much as necessary and do so openly. Nonetheless, it would be best if you expressed your disapproval in a kind and dignified manner.

When a leader disapproves, it is crucial to keep in mind that he is criticizing the opinions of the other speaker, not the speaker. For this reason, a leader should never reply by disparaging another individual personally. Therefore, he might offer an alternative perspective on the same problem rather than declaring that the speaker is foolish for approaching it that way. That demonstrates a leader's respect for another person's personhood even when they disagree with their beliefs.

Permit conversation.

That is the foundation of effective communication. A leader must listen to others. Refusing to give people a chance to speak does not diminish them. That never gets noticed, and it makes others more hostile toward you. People will view you as an autocrat rather than a leader. Your charm will wear out, and eventually, the public will turn their backs on you.

Taking Charge of the Discussion

As a leader, you need to be able to advance a topic through effective communication. We refer to this as conversation facilitation. Since it entails completing the agenda in a specific amount of time, discussion facilitation is essential in leadership situations. As a result, the company advances. The leader must prevent the discussion from stalling because this would result in unresolved business losses for the company. In actuality, this is what occurs when proceedings in national parliaments come to a standstill because the speaker of the house is unable to persuade the opposition and the government to agree on a matter. Therefore, a leader who is also an effective communicator must guide the conversation through an agenda.

Make an agenda.

You are the team leader and the meeting facilitator. Before every meeting, you should complete your assigned reading and arrange the things on the agenda. You determine which topics need to be covered and ask the team members to add their thoughts as well. After everyone has submitted their agenda items, you must rank them in order of importance to ensure that the most crucial ones get addressed first.

Plan the schedule.

All participants strongly detest drawn-out meetings. These gatherings reveal the flaws in the meeting facilitator. It demonstrates that the meeting's moderator does not influence what happens. As a result, the meeting's conclusion time must be decided by the leader. This is crucial since it enables team members to schedule their own time following the conclusion of the meeting. The next step is to prepare the discussion time for each item on the agenda according to the priority you have assigned to it.

Could you give it a go for everyone?

It is your responsibility as the leader to lead the discussion so that each person can speak. This accords each meeting participant their rightful prominence. When you are offering everyone an opportunity to participate in the meeting, you need to handle members skillfully. It will be necessary to motivate those who are inherently timid and reluctant to voice their opinions in front of others to do so. It will be required to exercise control over those who tend to speak excessively and monopolize the conversation. Both require tactful management; the assertive ones shouldn't feel like they are being repressed, and the timid ones shouldn't feel like they are going on an interview.

Observe the schedule.

Keep an eye on the clock and the agenda items to prevent the meeting from deviating into unrelated topics or tangents. Please make a note of these matters, as they might be significant and warrant discussion at a later meeting.

Supportive Attitude

A competent leader is always there for his group. Thus, having a supportive attitude is one of the social skills that a leader needs to master. Consider the position of a sports coach. Every player on the squad has skills and flaws that the coach is well aware of. In light of this, his role is to build on the team member's strengths and address their shortcomings in order to transform them into assets. We refer to a leader's twofold conduct as a supporting attitude.

People's strengths can only be enhanced by recognizing their other skills and giving them the chance to develop them. Therefore, if a teacher notices that a particular student is ahead of the class in most subjects, she might push him to go to more advanced themes or even begin working with him on the material ahead of time for the following year's class. This demonstrates to the pupil that while the teacher values his success, she still hopes he will reach greater heights.

Finding the obstacles in people's way and taking action to eliminate them is necessary to correct their deficiencies. Bottleneck removal is typically a process that takes time to complete. Sometimes, these obstacles have built up since a person's early years, making their removal challenging but not impossible. While trying to address areas of weakness, a leader must demonstrate patience. Providing the person with challenges of a comparable nature and having him solve them is one method of improving their deficiencies. It is possible to transform a person's flaws into strengths if they are persistent and the leader is patient. The willingness of the leader to address people's shortcomings instead of brushing them under the rug shows how helpful they are. It demonstrates that the leader cares about the success of his followers and wants them to reach new heights.

5: Managing Your Money for Financial Success!

Many individuals attempt to ignore the importance of this final pillar, but it really is crucial. Note that we are not advocating for financial abundance as a prerequisite for success. To be able to live a prosperous life, you must have a healthy economic vitality, and you must understand what financial health is. We'll delve deeper into the definition of economic health and how you might strive to get it in your own life to maximize your chances of success.

Unsteadiness in the budget and its effects on the economy may be excessive due to its illness or spillover effects to other areas of the economy. It could lead to a budgetary emergency that would be detrimental to the economy. For this reason, having a strong, stable, and stable monetary system is essential to supporting the efficient distribution of resources and management of risks throughout the economy. Additionally, it lessens people's tendency to get anxious in the event that the economy is negatively impacted and helps them feel confident about their place in the world.

To help you grasp the procedure better, let's take a closer look at this. Promoting and maintaining fiscal and monetary stability is one of the main goals of national banks since it supports a stable economy and manageable growth. By preserving the peace of financial institutions and the ability of the money supply to withstand adverse economic cycles and shocks, many banks absolve themselves of the responsibility to promote a sound and efficient monetary system. This prevents excessive disruptions to the intermediation process and maintains the stability of the financial system. This is crucially achieved by actively promoting the development of efficient budgetary markets, ensuring the continued dependability of actual payment and settlement systems, and regulating and overseeing accredited financial institutions.

To this end, significant resources are allocated to the establishment of robust reconnaissance systems that aim to identify weaknesses and support proactive measures to avert systemic unsettling influences.

As with any goal, developing excellent financial habits is necessary to stabilize your finances and become financially successful. In the past few years, a lot of individuals have been asking general questions about my objective to reduce debt, increase my finances, and create financial stability for my crew. I'll talk more about each of these tendencies in my speech, but first, I need to give an overview of them so that we can understand them better. In no particular sequence, here are all the various items you need to have for good financial health.

Create a reserve account as soon as you can. This should be your first focus, especially if you currently need a sizable crisis fund. Make it the first bill you pay each pay period, and as a result, transfer a certain amount from your bank account to your reserve funds (try opening an online reserve funds account). Don't even consider this transaction; make sure it occurs every payday. The entire process needs to be automated, and saving should become a regular part of your monthly (or biweekly or whenever you get paid) schedule.

Regulate your impulsive purchasing patterns. For many of us, this is the most worrying issue. Driving, eating out, shopping, and making online purchases all put a significant strain on our finances, are the most prominent way for many individuals to break their plans, and are unquestionably ways to find oneself in dire financial situations. Before making a big purchase, weigh your options and make sure you truly need the item in question rather than merely desiring it. It would be best if you approached all of your assets with a healthy mindset. If you don't need to buy anything, don't buy it.

Evaluate your expenses and lead a frugal lifestyle. In the unlikely event that you have never kept track of your expenses, try figuring out how much you spend each month. After that, evaluate how you're spending your money and choose what you can cut or eliminate.

Determine which costs are necessary, then stop the rest. It could take some getting used to, but once you have a solid budget in place, you'll discover that it's a lot simpler to go forward and make the savings you want to make. You'll be able to succeed, and your financial situation will improve.

Invest in your future with resources. If you're young and have only recently started working or exploring the globe, you likely need to give retirement more thought. In any case, it's essential. Take action now, even if you think you can wait until later to plan for retirement. If you start in your 20s, it will be unique to see how your theories about whether grow. If you can, start by increasing your 401(k) to the maximum match offered by your employer. A Roth IRA is the best bet after that. Do a little research, but start working on it right away! Avoid procrastinating too long, as the more time you spend delaying retirement, the less you will have left.

Protect your family's safety. The first step is to save money for emergencies so that you will have the funds available in case something unexpected occurs. Obtaining disaster protection and drafting a will as soon as possible is imperative if you have a spouse and children! Examine additional protections as well, such as those for leaseholders or property owners. In order to ensure that your family is taken care of in the event that something untoward happens to you or another member of your family, keep everyone and everything safe.

Either pay invoices right now or in advance. One excellent habit is to pay your bills as soon as they arrive. Similarly, to a reasonable extent, try to convince your creditors to pay your invoices using automated discovery. If you are unable to, use your bank's online check system to schedule regular installments. In this way, the majority of your funding's general expenses are covered. Add a little extra each month if you are able to. In this manner, your bills may wind up being lower in the event of an emergency, and you won't have to worry if your finances are tight for one month.

Eliminate and stay out of debt. You must start a debt repayment plan Please list all of your duties and schedule them, beginning with the least significant at the top two and working your way down. When that happens, focus on the highest-ranking responsibility and invest as much as you can, even if it's just an extra $40 to $50 (more is preferable). When the amount is finally paid off, rejoice! At that point, add the total amount you were paying—let's say the least installment of $80 plus the additional $50, for a total of $130—to the base installment of the following most enormous obligation. Continue in this manner, adding to your debt as you go until all of your commitments are paid off. Although it could take several years, this is an essential and advantageous process.

How Ideas Improve One Another

A hierarchical approach is the result of philosophy. This implies that earlier concepts build upon one another indefinitely. We start learning in our early years and keep adding to it throughout our lives, layering knowledge on top of understanding and creating new connections along the way. For knowledge to be sound, reality needs to be at the base of the pyramid.

Ideas originate from this layering. Simply put, concepts are collections of things. We can recommend someone you are familiar with. Though you can see him, you are unable to identify him as the "father." This idea is about a man who has given birth to a child.

It is based on what you already know and have encountered in life. It is crucial to keep in mind that the idea has a real-world counterpart. It has a place to begin. We are able to think about higher things because of concepts. We would not be able to learn more about the cosmos if we had no words for things like "father."

Concepts also include numbers. You cannot point to the idea of "fifteen" anywhere in the world, just like in the example above. It is hard to keep all that in mind, even if you can point out thirteen birds on a wire. An idea for the entities in their location is represented by the number "15." The higher functions of the brain are not possible without the notion.

Which idea do you find easier to remember?

instead

The birds need to be counted, which takes time. Any fifteen objects can be referred to by the idea "15," which is unrelated to the birds. It's an idea.

To emphasize this, philosophy must be grounded in reality and employ reason and logic to create a hierarchy of knowledge in order for people to navigate the world properly.

A manager's life has a beginning.

You are currently in a pivotal stage of your career as a manager. The abilities that brought you this far are not the ones that will advance you. People progress because they perform a task well. When it came to your work, you were the fastest and most proficient.

That's fantastic, but how does it help you in your new position? It's now clear to you. Now, instead of working quickly, you must guide others. Most promoted individuals merely attempt to use their prior knowledge to do tasks more quickly in their new roles. You are not in your new role for this reason. It is your responsibility to assist and equip them to execute their work rather than to perform it for them.

Your universe begins when you are born, just like the backdrop of your new role. At your company, it is the same. Your career begins the moment you step foot on the job. You don't know why anything happened or what came before. Some have been there longer and, depending on when they began, have a different perspective. Although those who join your team after you don't understand will need help understanding your background, everything influences how you approach your job. Everything was done with a purpose. Those justifications might not apply today. Before you jump in and start pulling things apart, find out; otherwise, you can end up doing more harm than good.

Ongoing Improvement

Being a leader is a self-directed path that calls for ongoing education and career development. The goal of continuous improvement is to raise the standard, which affects all facets of leadership. You work hard in your position every day to enhance the experiences of your coworkers, clients, patients, internal and external matrix partners, your goods, the way you provide patient care, etc.

Even while you can't alter the course of history overnight, the little adjustments you make over time will have the most significant influence and shape your legacy. Consider every day and circumstance as a chance. Try to leave things in a better state than when you found them.

Making significant changes that result in noticeable improvement takes time. Planning and principles of change management are necessary for this modality. In the end, if your goal is to implement significant changes rapidly, you will need to condition the team, adjust, and make sure quality controls are in place. This is a different thought process. If this is your objective, see the section on change management.

Continuous improvement and quality control are essential to the long-term viability of any firm. Quality control makes sure that items are produced at a level of quality that is either consistently high or higher than before. Furthermore, there's less chance of errors. Safety-syringe engagement is one instance of a situation in the healthcare setting where ongoing quality is expected. When using a safety syringe, you anticipate that it will correctly activate its safety mechanism to stop unnecessary sticks.

A continuous process aimed at enhancing goods and services is called continuous improvement. More minor changes could be made to increase productivity or cut out procedures that don't offer value. These enhancements might also be substantial, resulting in a total process redesign. One clinic, for instance, sought to reduce collections. The amount of supplies was significantly decreased by making a slight adjustment to the office process for getting payment from patients while they were in the clinic.

Six Sigma and Lean Healthcare both provide a wealth of tools. Spend a moment becoming familiar with these ideas.

Let's focus on continual improvement from a leadership perspective for the time being. What will set you apart from your followers in the end is your willingness to grow and learn. Recognize that being a leader is a journey, not a destination when you assume this responsibility. With time, your leadership skills will continue to develop. It's your job to tend to the road.

Chapter 11: Have Faith, But Check

A number of employees approached me in 2012 after a business Town Hall when we talked about the responsibility of our team to maintain safe working practices and the safety of our workforce. This was typical. People who felt more at ease asking questions in a private setting would typically seek me out after the lively Q&A sessions that concluded the Town Halls. The magic frequently occurred during the "side conversation," and I had the chance to learn what other people were thinking.

In one case, eight employees gathered around me, and the group leader announced that he would like to ask me a question on the group's behalf. Since I valued these exchanges, I replied in the affirmative. "Carson, you just told the whole workforce how important employee safety is to you, right?" asked the group leader.

I knew right away, based on years of experience, that the inquiry was a set-up by the group. With confidence, I responded in the affirmative, looking around to see how the others were responding. The leader then posed the query—or rather, the challenge—that he wished to bring to the group's attention. "So how do you think people will be focused on working safely when we have to work seven days a week for two months straight without a break?" he asked. We are humans, not machines, and with that kind of work schedule, we cannot maintain a safety focus.

I had my ear to the ground. Though I am aware that there are always some good issues brought up during these exchanges, this meeting and the questions were both a set-up and an ambush. Over time, leaders should learn when to confront a crisis rather than walk away from it. In this interaction, Having over 15 years of experience directing firms, I had a keen sense of what was going on.

I told the group leader and his staff that I understood their concern, and they both just gazed at me, waiting for my reaction. With a day off, working seven days a week would be a manageable schedule. I informed them that our sector could require some rigorous work patterns at some times (such as during drug shortages). I reminded them of the time when the United States was experiencing a flu outbreak, and we had to work incredibly long schedules to make sure that everyone could get vaccinated. I also reminded them that even in this extreme scenario, after the first month, we were able to hire more staff and reorganize the shift structures in order to decrease the workload.

After that, I promised the group that I would look into their inquiry and come back to them with an answer.

I had a gut feeling that their claim and criticism were either unfounded or out of context. Likely, you have also come across a circumstance or narrative with dubious facts. Furthermore, the majority of us have heard a story and taken the "facts" at face value, only to come to regret it later.

Because of Google, social media scams, and the sudden labeling of content as "fake news," we are now more likely to verify the integrity of tales we hear outside of work. What about internal work, though?

I've heard both true and made-up stories told to me by people in a variety of organizational positions throughout the years. As an individual who maintains confidence until it is betrayed, I have had to deliberately concentrate on identifying stories that necessitate fact-checking inquiries. Furthermore, I'll be honest with you—I'm not always correct!

I got a list of the eight employees' names and asked HR to compile an overtime report for each of them that afternoon. It turned out that only one person on the crew had worked a Saturday shift when I got the news later that day. In addition, two of the staff members had only returned from a five-day vacation the previous week, right before they confronted me about their work schedule.

This was a prime illustration of never letting the truth get in the way of a compelling narrative or of seizing the chance to ambush the leader and grandstand briefly. When I went out into the team's workspace the next day, I saw the group leader. We discussed it in a conference room. I followed up on the question he had posed to me in front of his staff and assured him that my dedication to ensuring the safety of our workers remained the top priority.

As I gave him his crew's work plans for the previous two months, I noticed him adjusting uneasily. I responded, "I want to understand your team's motivation for the situation that you initiated yesterday," while he was reading the report. I could tell that my follow-up took the group leader because of his hesitation.

Purpose provides an answer to the fundamental query of why your company even exists. We had a brief conversation about this last night at the pub. To make a living, each of us needs to do something. The majority of us select a skill, career, or employment to support different established groups. We perform our own SKERT analyses and work to get paid as much as possible for the skills we have.

Organizations must provide more than just a paycheck if they want to get the most out of us. If someone believes in the mission of the organization they work for, they will be more engaged. When we understand the organization's goals and align with its values, we also become more involved.

Businesses that do more for their workers than hire them have a competitive advantage. In the modern world, nearly every good, service, or method can be imitated. People travel around, and access to a wealth of knowledge is superficial. But, a company's strong employee engagement cannot be replicated. People are too complicated, and every organization has a different engagement strategy. However, the first step is to have a noble goal that people feel is meeting a need in the world.

Because capitalism is inherently unequal, it has a negative reputation. While it undoubtedly contributes to inequality, it is also arguably the most equalizing institution in recorded history. The importance of taking risks is something that some individuals need to realize. The only way society gets better is when creative people take out second mortgages to launch their businesses. Only some people are willing to take the necessary risks to establish a firm. We will only have new enterprises if we compensate those who just so happen to succeed.

If they believe in the goal of the company, the majority of employees are content for their owners to get wealthy. I've observed some workers taking satisfaction in increasing their owners' wealth. However, I've also worked in companies with greedy owners and disgruntled, disengaged staff. Which companies, in your opinion, are doing better?

I have to believe in a company whose workers are content to increase the wealth of the owners.

Yes, in fact. So, Tom continued, the first step in building a community of engaged employees is to establish a common purpose. What do you think the National's goals are?

I founded this company to relieve veterinarians of the burden of having to pay exorbitant prices at neighborhood human pharmacies for compound drugs by providing them with pharmaceuticals from an animal health company. Small- or large-pet owners shouldn't have to shell out a fortune for the same medications that average-sized animals may acquire for a reasonable price. Making it more straightforward for animals to take medicine is a large portion of our business. Whatever it takes to convince the sick puppy to take his prescription, for instance, we can change the taste of the drug or turn it from a solid to a liquid. Similar to Mary Poppins.

Is your client an owner of animals or a veterinarian?

Both, Ryan stated. The veterinarian is our main client. Hospitals place orders with us, and they pay us directly. On occasion, though, we provide the medication straight to the owner of the animal. Even though we go via the veterinary facility, we still have to treat the animal owner like a consumer because if they are not happy, it comes back to us.

According to Tom, your goal may be as simple as making sure all animals have access to the drugs they require to maintain their health. If you are an animal lover, that is a significant purpose. A marketing type could make this seem more inspirational.

Ryan responded, "It's great." Something like this would help focus our workforce on the benefits we offer. We're rescuing animals from death!

Consider all the tales you could tell in relation to this goal. Pet owners are willing to work for free! With a joke, Tom said.

Ryan raised his hand to end the discussion. Tom, hold on. They are playing trivia about American history. I must do this.

What year was the American Constitution written? The moderator of the hotel trivia game questioned the speaker.

Oh, that's simple, Ryan remarked. One hundred and seventeen.

The moderator verified that 1787 was the correct response.

Well, Tom continued, I knew it was about then.

Ryan remarked that the Constitution is a beautiful document. Though innovative at the time, it established the rights and structure that have made our wonderful country what it is today.

Church Leadership: Distinguished By Lack OfServanthood

In this section of the book, we examine this trend through an analysis of Church history in light of abuses committed by the hierarchy. This may appear to present a dismal picture of Church history, and it is essential to study and comprehend it in light of the fact that proper leadership techniques are not being used. That is not to say that there haven't been appropriate leadership displays throughout church history. I also drew attention to a few appropriate cases. This section of the book, however, focuses on church leaders abusing their positions of authority and power.

We cannot examine Church history apart from the theology and tenets that shaped the Church at different times.

Thus, throughout this section of the book, several theological and doctrinal questions are discussed. This is essential to comprehend how the Church's history has resulted in the blending of many concepts such as theology, leadership, power, etc.

History makes a fantastic teacher. I have purposefully created a terrible and bleak image of the mishandling and abuse of authority and leadership roles throughout our history by emphasizing specific incidents in this section. This is not intended to diminish the honor owed to all of the martyrs who endured great hardships and even lost their lives in order to propagate the gospel throughout the globe. Father Tertullian of the Church said in the second century that "the blood of martyrs is the seed of the Church," and his words still hold today. But whenever authority and status have been linked to leaders, there are many examples of their misuse, and as new leaders, we must be aware of this. Great men and women have stumbled in the past, and there's a good chance that you and I will succumb to the same temptations they did. Therefore, I'm hoping that these chapters that highlight the negative aspects of our Church's past may serve as a warning to us the next time we feel tempted to rely too much on our status, influence, and authority to get things done.

This section of the book mainly draws from Dr. Frank A. James III's recorded audio lectures on the History of Christianity I and II at the Reformed Theological Seminary. The seminary makes this tape accessible to the general public on their website.3. This work also incorporates unquoted additional allusions from a variety of sources, including Confessions of St. Augustine, Eusebius, Letters of Ignatius of Antioch, and Justin Martyr.

7) The professional

He continues on his journey like a train. He won't even respect your position if he can get by you and become more visible.

In order to progress in his job as quickly as possible, he will constantly be searching for new challenges or responsibilities.

Motivated resources are free to work hard as long as they respect responsibilities and don't bring problems to the team, with their attitude only focused on getting a personal advantage.

8) Your preferred

You want every employee in your company to be just like him. Always on time, accurate in reaching deadlines, courteous, situationally adaptive, and role-respecting.

You look at him and recognize the younger version of yourself, and you care about his career and well-being.

Make every effort not to display this preference in front of other workers. If you have to shower him with praises, do so privately rather than in front of others to avoid embarrassing him.

9) The trainee

A sponge that picks up knowledge quickly and can learn anything. Frequently, very willing and helpful.

Try to present him with some general guidelines for how to operate without forcing him to perform a task that does not allow him a minimal amount of freedom of action or alter him in any way.

10) The indifferent

You can't arouse him in the manner that you desire. He is naturally motivated. Therefore, you won't notice it in him. Ascertain that there are no issues with you, your job, or your coworkers, but don't be overly concerned about his persistently apathetic state.

11) All-around talent

He must constantly speak in an overly sentimental tone when making a point, regardless of the topic.

Try to explain to him that, for the most part, there is no scientific theory to back up what he is claiming.

You need to break down his ego, get him to start doubting himself, and teach him to take criticism. It will be a drawn-out but essential procedure.

12) The tense

is never able to make a decision or take a stand. He is going to be glued to you or anyone who even slightly seems trustworthy.

He will never accept a responsibility that even slightly raises the possibility of danger.

Try motivating him by gradually giving him more challenging assignments. It goes without saying that this road needs to be gradual; otherwise, the outcome you were hoping for would not materialize.

13) The impervious

He is the CEO's or President's closest friend. He is tough to manage because you can't criticize him, and anything you do or say could be used against you.

Even though you may wish to never deal with this kind of employee, avoid giving them special treatment as it will throw off the team dynamic and damage your reputation.

When using this kind of resource, you have to strike a careful balance, which frequently requires making concessions: you have to try to minimize the harm.

Eliminate anything that could be detrimental to the group's motivation.

As a leader, it is your job to make sure that the working environment is conducive to working. However, now and again, you may encounter situations that may affect the motivation of your followers in the wrong way. It is common, for example, for you to find members of the group who are negative thinkers. When negative thinkers shout out their opinions, they usually affect diminish the motivation of the individuals around them. Sometimes, people who are going through a rough phase in their lives may also create a sense of negativity in the group.

Getting rid of these individuals is a wise move to stop them from negatively impacting the group's motivation. You could also fire persons who tend to diminish the basis of the group. If this is not possible, at least limit their interactions with the other members of the group that you are leading.

Encouraging SustainersFor Prolonged Tasks

One of the biggest problems facing leaders is keeping their people motivated. According to studies, people are typically driven by three things:

The necessity of survival and safety

the yearning to fit in with a group of people

the requirement to fulfill one's potential

When pursuing the third need at work, employees are most focused on their work. Achieving the first and second needs is simple. Usually, after these demands are met, we cease working.

However, the third need necessitates a longer time frame or involvement. People who strive for this degree of personal growth do so in order to achieve mastery of their craft and autonomy. They also want to make a significant contribution.

Make sure your followers are striving for this degree of improvement if you want them to be inspired over the long term. If you are able to accomplish this, you will observe a rise in follower engagement.

The following advice will help you get your followers more involved in the tasks you want them to complete:

Give your followers the impression that they are acknowledged.

If the leader gives them a sense of recognition, people are more eager to join the group. Knowing the names of each follower is the simplest method to accomplish this. Persons are more likely to feel valued if you know their names. They will like you if you use this easy trick. They have a genuine sense of belonging to the company as a result.

One way to achieve this is to assign assignments to each of your followers based on their ability level. Remind them of their accomplishments if they perform well.

Look for ways to gauge and honor the work that those who follow you do. One way to express your gratitude to them is to thank them directly for participating in the organization's activities. You may also convey to them the significance of their work to the company.

Assign your followers a task based on their interests and skill levels.

When the tasks assigned to them do not align with their interests and skill level, people tend to become disengaged from their professions. A talented person will quickly become disinterested if you assign them a task that is too simple for them. They'll merely finish the assignment soon so they can move on to something more engaging.

Ensure that the individuals you hire have realistic expectations for the work they will be performing from the outset of the recruiting and recruitment process. If they are informed about the company's circumstances and compensation plan right away, they will be more likely to be involved.

Workplace Importance of Emotional Intelligence

In the workplace, emotional intelligence is more than just a passing trend that gets people excited. Employing emotionally intelligent workers has real advantages.

Employees with Emotional Intelligence Manage Pressure Better.

The workplace has evolved along with the workforce, which is distinct from that of the past. Workplaces used to be more laid back in the past. Today's employment is more competitive and demanding. Hiring managers are aware that workers who possess emotional intelligence will be more suited to succeed in high-pressure work environments. This is a result of their capacity to control their emotions, especially under trying circumstances. Imagine working in a setting where staff members are unable to control their emotions. When a critical deadline approaches, what is likely to happen? Most likely, there was a lot of scapegoating and shouting. This is undoubtedly a prescription for failure.

Employees with emotional intelligence make better decisions.

Making decisions is a daily task in the business sector. Aside from choosing which clients to pitch to, it would be best if you also decided which colleagues to include in specific teams, how to format reports for clients, how to manage your workload effectively, and a host of other issues. You are better able to make wise selections the more emotionally knowledgeable you are. Making non-emotional decisions is possible when you have learned to control your emotions. While emotions have their place, they are typically not the best drivers for making decisions.

For example, suppose you are a team leader, and you are tasked with completing a project for a client. One of your coworkers excels in conducting financial due diligence, which is a necessary talent for this project. Unfortunately, for reasons that are best known to them, this coworker does not truly like you. They have been so blatantly disrespectful in public that it is evident. How about you? Someone with low emotional intelligence could be tempted to argue with this coworker and exert control over them. Regardless of their differences, the team leader should be respected by their colleagues.

But, if you possess emotional intelligence, you will find a solution to handle the coworker as you understand that arguing with them would only impede the team's advancement. You will work out how to lead the team without providing them with a toolkit that they may use against you. Rather than engaging in their game, you will mercifully murder them. You'll be totally committed to living up to your potential and won't let that coworker bring you down to their level. This is a result of your internal motivation, self-awareness, self-control, and social skills, which are essential for managing a coworker who is acting like a whiny child.

Workers with High EQ Resolve Conflicts More Effectively

The office is a gathering place for diverse characters. Various personalities will likely clash when they get together. Not every time will coworkers get along. Even with staff parties or potlucks every other weekend, disagreements and strife among the workforce will persist. It is essential to have workers who can settle disputes amicably when there is disagreement.

Elevated EQ Workers Are More Enthusiastic

Assume for a moment that you are a company owner who has put a lot of effort into developing your brand and hiring a respectable staff. You believed in your vision and goal so much that you used your life savings to launch your business. Two years after you hired them, you begin to notice that every single one of them is arriving late, taking their time delivering work to your clients, and occasionally not turning up at all. Your brand begins to deteriorate. Your customers are no longer happy. You experience defeat. What went wrong, and where? Employees you hired needed more emotional intelligence.

Workers with Higher Emotional Intelligence Handle Criticism Better.

Consider having a staff member who pouts whenever they receive criticism. And how annoying would that be? Employers need more time or energy to deal with workers who take criticism personally. Emotionally intelligent workers are aware that they will occasionally need to be corrected. Their sense of self and value are independent of what their supervisor thinks of them. They are confident in who they are and receptive to criticism of any kind. Employers gain from having emotionally intelligent supervisors in addition to regular staff. These managers are more adept at leading teams, outlining the company's mission, and even resolving disputes. A manager with a low EQ could be the reason behind the company's demise. Such a boss will use threats, intimidation, and other unjustified methods to attempt to impose their control on the other staff members. This also applies to everyone else in a management role at work, including C-suite executives.

The Value Of Compassion

Being empathetic requires the ability to place oneself in the position of another. When you are compassionate, you are able to comprehend the other person's perspective and the reasons behind behaviors that may have appeared generous to them.

With empathy, we communicate with others in a caring and courteous manner and comprehend them when they speak to us. It is a powerful thing and the cornerstone of solid social interactions.

If empathy isn't something you naturally have, what techniques could you employ to start feeling other people's emotions?

We are all designed to have some degree of empathy for other people most of the time. Our brains are programmed to experience the emotions that other people are experiencing. That's why we wince when someone whacks their hand with a hammer or why we can't help but chuckle if someone else is doing it.

Regretfully, genuine natural empathy is a rare quality in people. Our ability to empathize is not constant. Some people possess a remarkable degree of perception and can tell how someone else is feeling just by glancing at them. Some people are not very empathetic, and they won't know you're upset until you start screaming. The majority of people are in the middle and seldom are able to sense the emotions of others.

Empathy is a skill that may be improved with the appropriate work and commitment. Depending on one's innate aptitude in this area, it can require more or less work, but anyone can develop their empathic abilities with the correct instruction and practice. That's exactly what this tutorial is meant to assist with.

This section is here to demonstrate how as well.

There are three lessons in empathy:

Recognizing Yourself

Recognizing Other People

Nonverbal Compassion

Recognizing Yourself

Understanding others' emotions is an essential skill for social cooperation. You'll be able to be a better friend and form stronger relationships if you have an understanding of other people's thoughts and emotions.

Nevertheless, it would help if you learned how to feel for yourself before you can learn to understand others.

That strikes me as having a really delicate inclination. This is profound and incredibly real-world. To be able to empathize with yourself, you must first be able to understand and recognize your feelings as well as the reasons behind them.

You should be able to remember "I feel irate" and understand the causes behind your anger if you're feeling angry. You must acknowledge and validate your emotions rather than suppressing or ignoring them.

At the most basic level, it should be acceptable for you to feel sorry for yourself if something dreadful happens. You have every right to feel sorrowful. We sometimes feel like we always have to be happy or that other people's problems are more important than our own, which makes us feel silly when we're unhappy or depressed.

That is invalid in any scenario. You matter, so your problems matter. Furthermore, it's acceptable to express your resentment and give yourself permission to experience your discomfort if anything is happening to you that makes you feel flawed or wounded. That doesn't need to be controlled.

Options for Meals

Bhakti texts tell us that taste is the first step towards serving. A child's eating attitude is essential since every bite feeds the cells with nourishment and positivity. Everything that has to do with food should be done with purpose. Through various grace-filled and grateful prayers, these meals are presented to the Inner Parents. Bhakti meals are vegetarian and filled with kindness and compassion for animals because of this. The act of preparing, serving, sharing, and consuming food is a whole spiritual practice.

You reply, "Our mealtimes are nutty," though. "You have to! I don't want to eat that!" was followed by, It's not sufficient to have ice cream and Cheerios for breakfast. I was shocked to find, as a new mother, just how difficult it was to get my children to eat the food I made! This is the ideal area to make choices that will transfer the energy because it can be a tiring effort. Apply your imagination. Give them options they will love. Pasta in a hearty tomato sauce with vegetables. Pizza flatbread topped with cheese and vegetables. Curry vegetables served with naans or chapatis. Beans and vegetables in tacos and enchiladas.Corn, potatoes, and bread. Vegetables buried within objects also function. Discover a few go-to healthy food options that are popular in your culture. I'll stop there because there are tons of information available online to assist you in helping your child eat healthily.

Their meal selections will increase if you ask them to assist you in the kitchen with meal preparation. My boys had the good fortune to study horticulture every week at school. They enjoyed helping me cook and learned so much. Children as young as five enjoy assisting in the kitchen. They most likely already have a basic kitchen set, complete with Velcro vegetables that they can chop and "prepare." Commence them as soon as you can. Please include them in the process of buying groceries. We intend to create a menu. Then, on the weekend, we'll go to the supermarket and get the essential ingredients.

Don't push them to eat anything if they are adamantly opposed to it! Anything that needed to be deeply chewed, like a salad made of lettuce, tomatoes, and carrots, was disliked by my elder child. It eluded my understanding. His molars weren't aligned, as we discovered years later when we viewed an impression of his teeth at the orthodontist! He could not even chew very rough food, such as lettuce. It wasn't only a matter of defiance. He was too young to tell me why he couldn't eat such things, so I felt horrible for making him eat something he couldn't chew. Remember to respect your child's innate preferences. And offer them options based on their interests. If you decide to work with me, I can assist you in navigating the demands of your particular child.

One thing to keep in mind is to make sure the options you're providing are appropriate. Guide them rather than give them free rein. Since they are still too young to make a decision based on long-term benefits rather than short-term ones, they might decide to eat mac & cheese every day if given the option.

A REACH FOR THE GROUND

During my early twenties, I had no intention of pursuing further education. As a result, I should have seized the chance the service presented to earn a college degree. When I found out that many employers would not speak to me because I did not have a degree, reality set in after I left the Marine Corps. My aspirations were dashed, which resulted in frustration after disappointment after disappointment. I got back into the fire department and worked hard to earn a business management degree. I obtained a master's degree because I wanted to become a chief officer and was looking to the future. I was admitted into the Executive Fire Officer Program at the National Fire Academy three years after being promoted to battalion chief. My expectations were high, and at that time in my life, my preparation and thoughts were focused on the next tier of chief officer jobs.

The chance presented itself in 2013 when I was selected as one of three finalists for a position as division chief of operations in a nearby department. Four distinct interview panels were held the next day after the candidate meet-and-greet with the fire department, a telephone interview, and a tour of the department led by the battalion and fire chiefs (i.e., another discussion). I was pleased with the procedure and eagerly awaited hearing from someone to find out if I had been hired.

The fire chief answered the phone and apologized, saying, "I'm sorry to tell you, but you didn't get the job." Whoa! Like three tons of bricks, it struck me. It was not just deep disappointment that came to the surface. Rejecting, not believing, failing, frustrated, and feeling a variety of other emotions. My hopes crashed to the ground like a meteor.

But there's still more. A division chief of operations post became vacant in my department two weeks before the last interviews in the neighboring department. Since I firmly believe in upholding honesty, I determined it would not be appropriate to leave one procedure and join another. After receiving a call of denial from the nearby fire chief, I called my head to inform him of the situation. I also promised him that I would look at the opening in our department. The interview was conducted with another battalion head and me two weeks later. The fire chief called me about three hours after my interview and said, "I'm sorry to tell you, Rick, but you didn't get the job."

THE EMOTIONAL DISAPPOINTMENT STORM

Whoa! Within two weeks of each other, there were two rejections for the same kind of job. My emotional meter was reading dangerously high. I thought I was a complete failure and wondered what was wrong with me. What would my shift's men and women think? Would they even believe that I could lead them anymore? Would they consider me to be unworthy? Would the department disregard me as unimportant? After all, I completed the Executive Fire Officer Program at the National Fire Academy and worked hard to obtain two degrees. In less than two weeks, my aspirations of becoming division commander were abruptly dashed,

Luckily, everyone on my shift—men and women alike—was incredibly encouraging. Some avoided me because they were unsure how to interact with me or what to say. It was probably just embarrassment from not knowing how to handle the situation, not malicious intent. To make matters worse, I was admitted to the hospital four months later with severe renal failure and a cancer diagnosis. However, that is a tale unto itself.

The "super-secret-squirrel" aspect of our work and its complexities make our role as recruiters fascinating and sometimes frustrating. Still, we keep coming back because it's intoxicating and nearly addictive! We have the opportunity to influence the organizations we work for and lead them toward their ideal states. Furthermore, we work primarily in the background and without recognition. We are an odd breed, leading a bizarre existence.

I apologize to all, but especially to Shakespeare and William Wordsworth, for this ode.

As a cloud-based recruiter, I work alone and am never inside the circle—always on the outside as an observer. I enjoy observing people and getting to know them to the point where I've turned somewhat of a square;

But not entirely, since I was never far from anything—no, not altogether square;

Additionally, not a part of the group nor making the decisions, but rather a party to them and an advisor;

Constantly observing, examining, inquiring, gaining knowledge, and perceiving; nevertheless, it goes much beyond that. Influencing, directing, choosing, and occasionally rejecting.

While protecting my organization, its leadership, its procedures, and its policies, I also support my hiring manager client and help advance the business by pushing for decisions, driving for results, and delivering creatively. On the other hand, I occasionally break glass, but never too much and always for the greater good.

I don't always jump when they yell or ask, "How high?" I'm not afraid. I sometimes abide by the spirit rather than the text.

But hold on, I also support my candidates in another corner, making sure they succeed and have a bright future, putting them in the best possible position to alter the world and have the most influence on the organization—all without giving anything away;

I am constantly bouncing between the organization, the client, and the applicant. Aye;

More points than a smooth circle; more mysterious than a stuffy square; constantly on the outside and always inside, coordinating the three magical points;

Keeping the three in balance, occasionally separately, occasionally together, but always with me in the center: The Strange Life Triangle of the Recruiter.

We must strike some equilibrium between meeting the needs of our clients and also allowing them to understand the consequences of their requests. Additionally, there are situations when doing what they desire is not the best course of action; therefore, we must also assume the role of advisor or consultant and inform them of the consequences of their choice.

In a recent instance, this is what transpired: While conducting our search, the interim leader had the bright idea to have every member of his leadership team interviewed for the role he was filling. He wanted to interview five separate persons, which made it difficult and required about 40 meetings. The interviewer then expressed dissatisfaction to the HR director, asking, "Why do we have to interview eight people?" After we looked into it, the interim manager wanted to demonstrate a just procedure and ensure that everyone had an equal chance to receive comments. However, given the length of time, we determined that we had to exert influence, engage in negotiations, and devise a win-win scenario. The procedure was changed, and fewer employees were involved. However, we had to advise the acting manager of the possible consequences of his actions and offer an alternate approach. He was aware of it and OK with the suggested course of action, but throughout our work, there will be ongoing teaching and influence.

In another instance, one of our top leaders had nominated a candidate, and he was determined to hire that person under whatever circumstances. However, the applicant needed to make it easier to hire by constantly erecting obstacles and attempting to circumvent our evaluation procedure. "Why do I need to talk to this person?" and "Why do I need to complete the assessment?" were some of the questions they posed. The interview process was challenging in every way. We engaged our business's

HR team partners in a conversation. We informed and included other corporate leaders in the problem as well. We continued bringing people in, so they could all see how complicated it had gotten. It is our responsibility to alert the appropriate parties, highlight any red flags that emerged throughout the hiring process, advise them that this individual might not be a good match for the position or the firm, and share our past experiences with similar scenarios. However, you also need to consult and lay everything out on the table at the same time.

Additionally, it would help if you were adaptable. It's their choice in the end, but they must make it with complete knowledge and understanding. And it is our responsibility to ensure that their eyes are open.

Using Your Mind Vs Solving Problems

I thus requested him to set up a meeting with forty of his top employees from every department and reserve two conference rooms for a two-hour workshop as an experiment to demonstrate to him what I was attempting to get him to see.

He questioned, "Why two conference rooms?" "They fit in one," we say.

I informed him that I wanted them divided into two rooms equally but at random. I wanted them to focus on the issue that my client and the majority of the organization kept referring to as "the problem with the warehouse."

To put it overly simplistically, the issue with the warehouse was that the dispatcher—they'd tried a number of people in that role—would eventually find themselves at odds with the service team about who would get and distribute parts that the team needed for fieldwork.

The warehouse, according to the service team, disregarded their demands and requests, particularly the urgent ones. The warehouse also claimed that the service staff was making irrational requests and needed help understanding the warehouse's limitations.

The CEO and the managers of both departments had attempted numerous approaches to address this persistent issue, but they had yet to be effective. Each team suffered from low morale as a result, and each group placed the blame on the other.

On the designated day, the attendees were split up and directed to two distinct conference rooms located across the hallway. I proceeded to the front of the first room, where individuals surrounded a vast table. The CEO was present to watch. I briefly worried that my experiment with language and communication might not succeed, but it was too late to change my mind.

I explained to everyone in the room that their purpose for being there was to work on the warehouse problem and see if they could solve it by cooperating. I questioned what was going on since I noticed a lot of rolling of my eyes and heard some groaning.

One woman remarked, "We've been trying to solve this problem for years now." "How will two more hours help anything if it hasn't been resolved after years of trying?" asked a second man.

I wanted a show of hands to see who would still be willing to try, even if I understood the validity of what they were saying and how understandable their feelings might be. And the reason they eventually raised their hands was because the CEO was positioned at the rear of the room.

Good, I exclaimed. "I respect your willingness to attempt. When your time together is up, we'll check in to see how you went.

As I proceeded across the hall to the other group with the CEO, he didn't seem hopeful. The CEO took his spot in the back once again, and I moved to the front. I experienced another wave of worry upon realizing that this could be my final day of employment with him.

I told everyone in this room that I used to work for an advertising firm and that when we were pitching to an account, the creative department would frequently arrange a brainstorming session to generate ideas. When I inquired, a few of them explained what a brainstorming session was, but the majority didn't.

"It's meant to be carefree and enjoyable," I remarked. "The situation at the warehouse, which is now not operating, will be the main focus of this. One of you will take a position at the whiteboard and alternately circulate the room, offering suggestions for what should be written there. You can express whatever comes to mind; the ideas can be as bizarre and wild as you choose. You will feel foolish about some of your thoughts and not about others, but that doesn't matter.

All ideas will be treated equally as you proceed. At the conclusion, you will rank the pictures according to potential after looking at the board and voting on the three that you believe have the most possibility of succeeding. The only need is to have fun, be carefree, and not worry about the result in any way. I did not describe the state of affairs as a "longstanding problem." This was not apparent to the CEO when comparing the setup for the first group.

After they received the assignment, the CEO and I went into his office so that I could explain the information I needed him to view. I conveyed to him that employing oppressive, fear-driven language and communication would inevitably lead to fewer practical solutions being developed by his workers. I informed him that if the warehouse situation were consistently presented as a "serious problem that needed to be solved," it would remain in that concerning range. He remained dubious.

To what extent should you pursue your education?

Your desired level of proficiency will determine how many skills you choose to acquire. You'll need to invest more time in learning anything if you want to get great at it.

The two primary reasons I advise concentrating on mastering just one or two abilities are listed below:

You'll advance more quickly. Learning anything requires sustained focus and consistency over time. It is easier to understand when you are attempting to learn fewer things at once.

You'll acquire employable abilities. Education is a procedure. You can only fully comprehend a talent by applying what you have learned to its fullest. Attaining a high degree of proficiency can help you develop vital abilities like perseverance, self-assurance, and a better understanding of how learning occurs. Because of this, you'll be able to go over any obstacles, which will help you with any other skills you want to master in the future.

How much time a day/week should you dedicate to learning?

It would help if you chose how much time you'll spend acquiring the talents you want to achieve now that you have a more straightforward concept of what they are.

There's no simple answer to this because it depends on a lot of variables, such as how much time and energy you have to spare each day and how quickly you want to pick things up. But allow me to provide you with some general principles. Generally speaking, learners can be categorized into three groups:

Intermediate students (3–5 hours per week), advanced students (5–10 hours per week), and masters students (25–35 hours per week)

The key takeaway from this is that you should commit three to five hours a week, minimum, to learning any significant skill that can have a substantial influence on your life. Anything less than that is likely to be useless or take too long to obtain. Consider this: is acquiring a skill really that important to you if you can't commit at least three hours a week to it?

The snake went in search of food around dusk. However, it appeared that he was preoccupied and was playing around with the mousetrap. Later, what was the snake? Why was he fiddling with the mousetrap when he should have been out hunting food somewhere else?

A REAL-LIFE STORY:

Prominent pioneers possess a strong sense of focus. Have you ever started something with the intention of completing it but ended up doing something else instead? Why does something like that occur?

PRIORITIES VS. FOCUSES

 Making the best choice now is what is meant by centering; prioritizing is the desire to make the best selection first.

You must be very clear about your objectives. You are more likely to concentrate your attention on your goal if you know exactly what you want. Focus is only possible in the presence of purpose. Progress is accelerated by stress. Although it's challenging to achieve a perfect guide, you can practice it all the time.

'MOUNTAIN' METAPHOR

Concentration is like a mountain. Reaching the summit in advance is a challenging feat. However, with time, we can progressively ascend the mountain one step at a time. In a similar vein, we wish to prime our brains to focus. This is the mystery of the center. You can concentrate more freely the more you train yourself to center. It takes some initial investment, but in the end, it is profitable. You will achieve a state of "flow" where you are entirely absorbed in the task at hand when you can train your mind to focus on it voluntarily. That's when your productivity reaches its pinnacle, and you get to the summit of the mountain.

PRIORITIES OF ATTENTION

The majority of people need help with focusing. Identifying distractions is the first step toward being able to concentrate. Discover what's

preventing you from achieving the objectives you have set, and strive to reduce those distractions.

Here are three easy-to-implement center suggestions for you.

Turn off all sources of distraction if you are going to complete a significant task, including emails, social media, phones, alerts, and alarms. Shut down any unnecessary applications if you're using a computer.

If you have a brilliant idea for anything else while you're working, disregard it or quickly write it down on your "Do

Someday" list and carry on with the current activity.

Just assign call handling to someone else or send calls to voicemail if you are concerned that you will miss an important call while you are deeply engaged in your work. Additional choices include:

- Marking emails as read-only.

- Posting a "don't disturb me now" sign on your desk. or

- Putting an I'm busy status on your chat apps.

For instance, I have a status update on my messaging apps that says, "Can't talk now, but I love you." Most folks will return to me later after acknowledging that.

Recall this: Focus expedites development. You'll make more progress and feel more motivated to do more if you are more focused. It could be challenging to implement this right away because you're used to dealing with disruptions. Now, try your hand at getting used to focusing.

Best Training Protocol For New Employees Joining The Company

A novice who is accepted as a professional at a company may have a superficial understanding of corporate affairs due to their lack of experience with operational modes, inter- and intra-corporate relations, functional layout of the company, etc. Even their recognition of the organizational structure and work culture could be more specific. This implies that when engaging in company matters as an employee, one needs a comprehensive approach. The new hire needs some time to settle into their "niche" in relation to the company's growth vision, as well as the growth they envision for themselves.

When new officer joins a business, their training should be designed to provide them with a brief understanding of the work descriptions of their inline juniors and seniors. To ensure that the new hire grasps the fundamentals of their job profile and role within the company, it should be permitted for them to assist all seniors and juniors. It is essential to inform the novice on both intra- and interdepartmental roles, as well as their potential areas of work and limitations. In this manner, the newcomer would quickly integrate into the corporate structure and begin contributing to the creation of profits for the company. It is generally recognized culture that one will gain experience gradually, fit in with the workplace, and fulfill official duties gradually. Gradually? The company typically bears a latent cost of this lengthy procedure, and the new hire is doomed to make mistakes! Therefore, it is preferable to receive training in accordance with the corporate schema with regard to corporate affairs, operational modes, inter- and intra-corporate relations, and the functional layout of the corporation, all of which are aligned with the employee's contribution to the corporation. In this manner, potential errors (that the new hire might make while performing a task) can be prevented.

Psychological point of view: A person's cognitive capacity always takes in the information that is offered. In the subconscious mind, a new logic architecture is created in reaction to the stimuli. According to psychologists, the subconscious mind can be educated to influence conscious perception and exert control over conscious processes. The following talents develop as a result of the conceptualization of this psychological theory, which guides the appropriate training module for any human brain. As company executives, it is our responsibility to ensure that the new hire's training timetable makes sense and that errors in job execution only arise from a completed training program.

Business lesson: Corporate refers to a profit-making company. The human resource is a crucial component of the corporate foundation, responsible for overseeing commercial transactions and protocol execution. In order to prevent needless expenses for the company, hiring new personnel should follow a streamlined training program that puts them on par with the best (current) employees.

Important Phrases That You Can Use Right Now

Many circumstances look intimidating or uncomfortable, so we steer clear of them altogether. But what should we do when we have to face challenging situations like asking for a pay raise or turning down a demanding person? I've outlined several adequate words and techniques for achieving our goals in this section. Try out the questions, strategies, and ideas listed below; they are all meant to be used right now.

Getting Paid More

We all deserve a pay raise, including you. People are overworked and underappreciated far too frequently; the issue is that most people take this seriously. Like most things, asking for a pay increase might be intimidating, but the secret is to know what questions to ask. The technique for asking for a pay raise that is outlined below is incredibly effective and has a high success rate.

Select your battlefield.

Don't just blurt out in a team meeting, "I need more money!" Your best option will be to ask to have a private conversation with your manager. Don't waste your time and jump directly to the top; not all superiors can execute a pay boost. Make sure you're asking the proper person.

first inquiry

This initial request is more of a setup for the pivotal inquiry than it is intended to be approved.

QUESTION: "Thank you for your time today. You have always been very understanding of me, so I wanted to talk to you about a question. Could you assist me? I require a compensation increase. After that, pause.

Likely to respond

Requests for wage increases are something that supervisors and managers handle on a regular basis, so this is familiar to them. If they reject your request, it will be dismissed in one of the following ways:

"We don't have the money."

"Delay until the start of the upcoming fiscal year."

"We'll talk about it when you get appraised."

"I don't have time to talk about it right now."

Final blow

The killing blow may appear a little forward at first glance, and it is. Since this method of inquiry is unfamiliar to your supervisors, you should anticipate an open and encouraging response. Because your managers and bosses are decent people by nature and desire to be viewed as such, the killing blow will force them to choose between seeing themselves favorably or unfavorably.

"I've come a long way since I started working here. What do you think I'm worth?"

Your manager or boss may pause for a moment at this point, but the only practical course of action left to them is to validate your value and, thus, consent to a pay increase; I'll let you negotiate the specific figures.

The approach mentioned above has been tried and true and has consistently worked. Asking for a raise may need some bravery, but don't worry—you'll get what you want.

Take Full Advantage Of Your Skills

God has endowed us with special skills, aptitudes, and capabilities. They are a person's SHAPE, according to Rick Warren, and they include their spiritual gifts, heart, abilities, personality, and experiences. These assortments of skills are the unique gifts that God has given each of us, enabling us to be uniquely ourselves and different from others.

You've missed the purpose of life if you believe that your abilities are just something you'll use to amass wealth, settle down, and pass away. Your talents were given to you by God, not for your gain. And God bestowed onto others gifts that help you.

Every member of Christ's body matters since we are all a part of it. In the family of God, there are no minor individuals.

God is shaping you to serve him, and he is trying to see how you will use the gifts he has given you.

God gave you the skills to serve others, whether you are an accountant, teacher, singer, or chef. God has given you gifts, and you are in charge of managing them. Regardless of how big or small you think they are, God cares about them. First Corinthians 4:12. God invested in you when he created you, and he wants a return on that investment.

God wants you to use the abilities and skills he has given you to help others and improve the world rather than just yourself. God expects you to use the gift that he has given you. It resembles a muscle. It will expand if you utilize it. You will lose it if you don't. Similar to the parable of the ten talents found in Luke 19, God will take away what you have and give it to someone else who will use it.

2. Allow your leadership qualities to come through in your actions and words. Your words and deeds should always be in line with the actual state of the company. If an immediate overhaul is required, you must convey this urgency to your team and to everyone else you interact with. In addition, you must always act with optimism regarding the organization's future. Make wise choices that allow everyone to accept their position of authority.

Accept responsibility for your actions without assigning blame or offering justifications for why things occur.

Above all, accept the state of affairs as it is; try not to overstate or produce work that is too little or unimpressive as this will only set you up for failure. It's okay to start making significant progress toward the goal on the first day. It is acceptable to move cautiously, slowly, and deliberately. Lastly, make sure you get excellent outcomes.

3. Communication is critical: If you believe you communicate enough, you've never held a leadership position in a company.

If communication is not effectively managed, misinformation, miscommunication, and misinformation are significant obstacles for any leader.

It is insufficient for a leader to speak once or twice; in order to make sure that the meaning of their message is being understood, they should talk three times as often as they would on an average day. In extreme cases, they should speak four or twenty times. Engage in communication with your team, set up in-person or virtual team meetings, and never, ever let your staff question your relevance or existence. Learn about them and introduce yourself, your guidelines, and your work ethic. Communicate information in a direct, concise, and understandable manner. Answer their inquiries, pique their curiosity, and insist on reports detailing each advancement the teams make.

Get together with every member of the group. You'll notice recurring themes that require discussion. In order to accomplish this, be sure to hold more one-on-one meetings with your team and find out about their individual reports' roles.

4. Set a clear precedent for your group: As previously mentioned, you have to show that you share every team member's level of commitment to the company's vision and goals through both your words and deeds.

You have to do this without giving it any thought or compromising, and you have to keep demonstrating how much work you and the team put into making the company successful.

By doing this, you will have an impact on other team members and inspire the individuals under your direction to work just as hard and be equally dedicated. It is not enough to direct and dictate to others; you should actively engage in the laborious tasks at hand.

5. Don't let emotion influence your team selection: Choosing the right team to lead the organization's operations is one of a leader's most significant duties. In order to do this, the leader needs to constantly be searching for people who will embody the company's values and vision and who will go above and beyond to support the company's expansion.

They have to be gifted, and in some cases, their objectives in life should coincide with those of the business. With it, you will have something to offer your company, and there will be a relationship between the work that your employees do and their jobs.

On the other hand, some people will disappoint even after a thorough selection process, or over time, their abilities, output, and talent will become obsolete. Please do not be reluctant to release them. If a member of a team is not improving, there's probably a problem elsewhere. Being a leader means having to be prepared to make the difficult choice to let people go. Although severing ties with people you hold in high regard won't be easy, you must ultimately prioritize the expansion of the company over the needs of struggling individuals who could impede its progress.

In conclusion, the ability to become a great leader lies at the core of how to succeed as a new one. In order to lead your team and organization effectively, you must set high standards for yourself, make sure you create a vision that is both exciting and challenging, and then translate that vision into practical plans of action and quantifiable outcomes.

Management academics have provided numerous definitions of leadership, some of which are as follows:

It is the act of persuading people to work voluntarily toward an organization's objective rather than against it.

A dynamic process occurs in a group when one person persuades others to help the group accomplish its goals. Ownership is a process as well as an attribute. The method is the application of non-coercive influence to guide and plan a group's actions in order to achieve its goals. As a property, leadership is the collection of traits or attributes ascribed to individuals who are thought to effectively use such influence.

It is a significant improvement above and beyond rote adherence to the organization's regular directives.

The definitions mentioned earlier demonstrate that leadership is a dynamic process and that influence originates with the leader who guides followers toward the accomplishment of objectives. However, since it was found that power in complex organizations comes from both the top-down and the bottom-up, the conventional wisdom that influence emanates from the leader has changed. For instance, the news editor might closely examine news reports from reporters who are thought to be incompetent. Still, she might need to pay more attention to those from more experienced and competent reporters. This demonstrates the impact a reporter's performance can have on a leader.

Once more, the news editor may permit a reporter's behavior by assigning him to stories that don't require a lot of face-to-face interaction with news sources. The news editor has the power to reassign or fire a reporter who is deemed impolite and indignant. He can force him to work more at his desk than on the field. These illustrations highlight the nuanced dynamics that exist between superiors and subordinates in media organizations, as well as how an organization's subordinates' attitudes can impact editors' leadership styles.

A manager with a formal position does not always have to be a leader, which is another aspect of the leadership process that needs to be understood. A leader, however, could be someone other than the news editor who motivates people to complete tasks, even though the news editor holds formal management authority in the newsroom of a newspaper company. The news editor stands out as a leader because of his capacity to motivate his reporters to perform their duties voluntarily. The official head of the department is indeed the formal leader, but the informal leader of the department is the one who shapes the behavior of their peers. The traditional leader only sometimes assumes everyday leadership, even though it is possible for the informal leader to be the formal leader.

It is important to note that department leader finds fulfillment in their roles and responsibilities due to the acknowledgment they receive from both lower-level staff and upper management. This group's refusal to acknowledge him could result in the withdrawal of his authority. This leads us to the idea of power and how it relates to the leadership process. In light of this, the manager and others must rely on their personality and expert power rather than position power alone.

Brokenness necessitates ongoing care.

You enter a state of initial brokenness or death when you give your life to Christ. However, there are probably still a lot of unbroken places in your life, and since brokenness is a daily process, you might only be living a partially surrendered life.

Jesus tells you to follow Him and take up your cross "daily" (Luke 9:23). You will have daily challenges to your own demise. These trials will occur when you interact with others rather than when you study your Bible. God tests your brokenness through other people. Perhaps He will use your nasty supervisor, your impolite coworker, the offensive remarks made by your spouse, or a rumor that has been spread about you. Whether or not you will walk in brokenness is revealed by how you react to these circumstances. Self-focus is demonstrated by defensiveness, rage, hurt feelings, self-pity, and shifting of blame.

A daily decision leads to this deeper life of death. I will never be delighted in Jesus until I turn from my sin and forgive my wife, even if I get upset with her the next day.

It's easy to think that your resentment and anger are justified because someone else violated your rights. It doesn't, though. Though He holds you responsible for your reactions to their actions, God does not hold you accountable for what other people do to you. Start viewing people as God's agents who are there to test you, rather than as your enemies.

The Impact Of Disintegration

Your entire life will be revolutionized by brokenness. When you are broken, Christ is free to work in and through you. Observer Nee states that the Spirit is released when the self is broken in his seminal book Release of the Spirit. He compares the self to a shell that encloses God's Spirit. The Spirit is limited as long as the self is present. However, the Spirit can manifest when the self is shattered. sixteen

Jesus showed that He was broken throughout His life and death. Jesus was the target of much slander, but He remained calm. He was hated by many, but They did not hate him. He never got angry, not even when He was tired. Despite people misinterpreting and misunderstanding what He said, He declined to defend Himself. He took the false charges silently. Jesus received power from His Father on a daily basis because He gave His life to the will of God.

Of course, the most obvious example of Jesus' death to himself is the cross. In the garden, Jesus surrendered, pleading, "Not my will but yours be done," even though He neither deserved nor desired this death (Luke 22:42). Christ calls you to imitate Him in the same manner, to be broken for Him as He was broken for you.

Disarray within the house

Your home is the most challenging place to practice brokenness because that's where you're most likely to reveal your true self. You take off your lovely "masks" at home. Your true self emerges at home, frequently in disagreeable ways. Would you be willing to have Jesus spend ten days living among you, silently observing everything you do? Probably not.

You will own up to your mistakes when you live in a broken home. You'll be the first to admit when you're wrong. Do you think I'm forgiven? You'll also be able to reprimand people with love. Frequently, harsh words of discipline directed at your spouse or children originate from unresolved sin in your own life. You will speak in love and discipline in love when you are correctly broken.

Furthermore, you will give up your "rights" when you are broken. You might think you're worthy of a calm, quiet evening. A husband might believe he has the "right" to eat at the same time every night or to be followed unthinkingly, even when his orders are absurd. A wife might believe that having the flexibility to manage her own schedule and receiving love and affection are her "rights." In Christian homes, there is conflict due to all these "rights." It's important to keep in mind that, as servants, we have no "rights." Give God your "rights" in genuine brokenness and discover how to live in harmony even when your "rights" aren't satisfied.

A broken leadership system

Your leadership is also profoundly impacted by brokenness. It allows you to take criticism without getting upset. Because no leader can win over everyone, criticism of the administration is typical. When someone questions you, how do you answer them? An unwavering leader turns tough and protective, frequently using his position to stifle dissent. A broken leader will listen intently, consider the situation carefully, and then make a decision. He will feel confident enough to adjust and even express gratitude to someone who has voiced valid criticism. He will stay on his path and still show love to the person in question, even if the complaint is unwarranted.

The shattered leader has a low opinion of himself. He may be a competent leader, but his brokenness keeps him reliant on God. He understands that in order for him to lead effectively, he needs the assistance of both God and other people.

A broken leader won't hesitate to give others praise and opportunities. Even when others' accomplishments surpass his own, he takes great pleasure in them since his goal is to advance God's Kingdom rather than his own. A broken leader is open and honest with others. He won't remain hidden behind pretenses and pretend to be a "super saint" who never considers sin. Since he acknowledges his struggles, he treats people who struggle gently. Instead of walking in contempt toward others, he walks side by side with them. He acts with kindness and love, even when his position requires him to take disciplinary action. A leader in brokenness helps others. Because the issues of pride and self have been resolved, he can do this without hesitation. The broken leader does not fight for a position or make an effort to impress people; instead, he is comfortable with who he is. This was demonstrated by Jesus right before he bent down to wash his disciples' feet. Because He understood who He was and what His father had called Him to do, He was able to serve His disciples. He had perished because of His own goals and plans.

These are the leaders that the world needs. People like these are what our homes need. The church is waiting for men and women who will follow Jesus' instruction to "die every day." Your company or school requires a good leader. Are you ready to pass away today? Are you prepared to let go of the parts of yourself that are still present in your life? Would you be willing to confess to Jesus, "I need to be cleaned?" I'm carrying a lot of myself with me. I can see it in how I treat other people, how I deal with authority, and how I treat my spouse.

Proceed now. Take action right now. Give yourself to Christ and allow Him to break you. He will then and only then be fully revealed in you. Spend some time in prayer and solitude with God, considering the lessons covered in this chapter. Finish the action assignment and make yourself available to God's desire to work in your heart. Compare the characteristics of broken and proud people.

Sincerely check the option on each line that most accurately characterizes you at this moment. In order for God to fully utilize you in His work, I pray that He will bring you to a place of personal brokenness.

How To Conduct Effective People Analysis

You need to be able to evaluate people in order to have any influence over them. Understanding people's needs will be highly challenging if you don't know who they are. People analysis can give you the knowledge you need to influence others or even comprehend them well enough to get along with them. The ability to decipher both verbal and nonverbal cues is necessary for people's analysis. Even though not everyone is logical, it is still possible to read people—but only with the correct knowledge and enough experience.

You can only fully understand others' needs or feelings if you are able to read social cues. As a result, you might need help to get along with others. Being vulnerable and opening up to new information is essential for influencing others. This can only be accomplished by letting go of your emotional baggage, ego, and painful experiences, as well as your preconceived notions. You have to be objective about people in order to understand and influence them, which means you have to stop passing judgment on them. By focusing on learning more about others and not on things you are holding onto or that prevent you from comprehensively analyzing people, you will be receptive to new information.

Who are you attempting to read for? It might be a stranger, your spouse, your coworker, your boss, or a friend. The key to analyzing people is to pay attention to details and gather sufficient data to make an informed decision. Reading someone entails analyzing them, which calls for the following actions:

Take note of body language.

Did you know that only about 7%, sometimes even less, of human communication is done through words? Our nonverbal cues make up 55%. Even the way we speak matters more than what we say because it shapes people's opinions of us in 30% of cases. This insight has led to the realization that the adage "It's not what you say, but how you say it" holds a lot of truth. That is true, not just something that Professor Albert Mehrabian, a wise man, once stated. Remembering this, it could be better to judge someone based solely on what they say when they speak. Instead, there's more information and significance to be gained from how they sound when speaking, and particularly from how they behave, appear, and use their bodies to convey meaning. It is unreasonable to judge someone—or be judged—just by the words that come out of our mouths when considering how we speak. Essentially, then, it is not possible to be excessively severe or analytical. It's preferable to keep calm and consider everything instead.

One way to do this is to take into account someone's appearance. Could you take a look at their attire? It's also essential to take into account their posture. They are confident if they hold their heads high. If not, there are a number of factors to take into account, such as the person's shyness, surprise, loneliness, melancholy, stress, embarrassment, and, of course, lack of confidence.

People's movements alone reveal a great deal about who they are. Their body language can indicate a number of things, such as their inclination, whether they cross their arms or legs, conceal or fidget with their hands, bite their nails, touch their faces or hair, or bite their lip. Ultimately, a person's facial expressions are the most expressive. There are two ways to interpret it: the first is by looking at how they react in the moment, which usually shows a glimpse of their feelings and thoughts, and the second is by looking at how their long-term emotions appear on their face. There are various ways to view these feelings. This includes deeply creased eyebrows that convey worry or overanalysis, crow's feet, which are also referred to as smile lines and gradually give joy, naturally pursed lips that give resentment, rage, and disdain, and clenched teeth or jaw that convey tension.

Embrace your instincts.

You communicate differently, both through your body language and your words, because you take into account other people's intuition when interacting with them. You can tell if someone is good or bad by feeling it in your gut. Now, while some people may possess a keen sense of intuition, others may not. It makes visible nonverbal cues that you pick up on when you observe someone or something closely and come to understand something about them. You can see beyond what is physically visible in front of you when you have intuition. It also helps you select more accurate intuitive cues, but in order to do this effectively, you need to ● Pay attention to your intuition, especially when you're meeting someone for the first time.

It typically presents the data you gather and your emotions before you have a chance to reflect and form an opinion about someone. After meeting someone, gut feelings can appear seconds or minutes later. It communicates whether or not you can trust people.

● Think about the goosebumps.

Despite its ridiculousness, goosebumps serve as an indicator for our intuition to tell us what resonates with us— including other people. Goosebumps can happen when we're scared, inspired, or even moved. It also occurs when you recognize things and moments or when you have a deja vu feeling with people.

● Watch for signs of intuitive empathy.

Anyone can have empathy. There are various scales associated with it, though. Some people have a small amount of heart that is typically underdeveloped, while others have a great deal of empathy—so much so that they can sense other people's feelings even when they are silent. Empathy allows you to read people. It calls for a certain level of selflessness as well as an increased awareness of your surroundings. Being empathetic will make it much easier for you to read people, whereas not being empathetic will make it difficult for you to connect with others and earn their trust.

● Take note of your wisdom.

Do you recognize those "ah-ha" moments that could pass you by if you don't pay attention to everything that is going on at all times? We all tend to miss insight because we are all preoccupied with too many things at once, particularly when it comes to our thoughts. For example, you might lose out on learning more and gathering information about someone in person if you are not fully engaged because you are preoccupied with other thoughts during the conversation. Distracted listening may cause you to miss far more than just what they are saying, especially since repeating someone else's words only accounts for 7% of the total information we could learn from them.

www.ingramcontent.com/pod-product-compliance
Lightning Source LLC
Chambersburg PA
CBHW071708210326
41597CB00017B/2396